The Story
of Anne Frank

by Stewart Ross
illustrated by Alan Marks

Thameside Press

Distributed in the United States by
Smart Apple Media
1980 Lookout Drive
North Mankato, MN 56003

Text copyright © Stewart Ross 2001
Illustrations copyright © Alan Marks 2001

Editor: Steve White-Thomson
Designer: Simon Borrough
Language consultant: Norah Granger, Senior Lecturer
    in Primary Education at the University of Brighton, U.K.
With thanks to Kay Barnham for her editorial help
    in the latter stages of this book.

Library of Congress Cataloging-in-Publication Data

Ross, Stewart.
    The story of Anne Frank / written by Stewart Ross.
        p. cm.
    ISBN 1-930643-20-9
        1. Frank, Anne, 1929-1945--Juvenile literature. 2. Jewish children in the
    Holocaust--Netherlands--Amsterdam--Biography--Juvenile literature. 3. Holocaust,
    Jewish (1939-1945)--Netherlands--Amsterdam--Juvenile literature. 4. Amsterdam
    (Netherlands)--Biography--Juvenile literature. [1. Frank, Anne, 1929-1945. 2.
    Jews--Netherlands--Biography. 3. Holocaust, Jewish
    (1939-1945)--Netherlands--Amsterdam. 4. Women--Biography.] I. Title.

    DS135.N6 F73555 2001
    940.53'18'092--dc21
    [B]   2001027258

Printed in Hong Kong

9 8 7 6 5 4 3 2 1

Introduction

It was the middle of May, 1940. World War II was raging in Europe. The Nazis had taken over Germany and attacked the countries around them. During the last few days, they had defeated the Dutch.

In the Dutch city of Amsterdam, a father and daughter were watching the enemy arrive…

The Trucks

The noise went on and on. Anne Frank let go of her father's hand and covered her ears. She stood back from the edge of the pavement and stared at the roaring stream of dark trucks. They were all full of soldiers.

When the last truck had gone around the corner, Anne lowered her hands. She looked up at her father. He was a tall, handsome man dressed in a neat, gray suit and brown hat.

"Is that the end of the war, Daddy?" she asked, feeling for his hand again.

Mr. Frank looked down at his ten-year-old daughter and smiled gently. Anne knew the look well. It said, "I am smiling because I love you, not because I am happy." He lifted his eyes and looked at where the trucks had been. "It is the end of the war for the Dutch. But it is not the end of the war for us."

Anne frowned. She didn't understand.

"Those soldiers were Nazis," her father went on. "They are in charge of the city now."

"But I don't understand what you mean," said Anne. "What do you mean?"

Mr. Frank checked to see that no one was listening. "Anne, we are Jews," he said in a low voice. "The Nazis hate all Jews."

"Then I hate all Nazis!" said Anne crossly.

Before she could say anything else, her father put his hand over her mouth.

"Never say that again!" he ordered.

Anne was shocked. Her father was normally such a gentle man. Why was he acting like this? She felt hot tears come into her eyes.

Mr. Frank took away his hand.

"I'm sorry, Anne," he said, bending down and putting his arm around her. "But you must be very careful what you say now. Just in case. Promise me?"

Anne quickly wiped her eyes on her sleeve. "Yes. I promise." When she looked up at her father's face, she saw something she had never seen before. He was afraid.

The Frank family were German Jews. The leader of the Nazis, Adolf Hitler, blamed the Jews for everything that went wrong in Germany. So when the Nazis took over Germany in 1933, the Franks moved to Holland to get away from them.

The Nazis treated the Jews very badly. Now the Nazis had invaded Holland, and the Frank family and other Jews who lived there were in real danger.

The Cloud

There was a strange silence in their apartment when Anne and her father arrived home.

Mr. Frank sat down at once and pretended to read the paper. Anne's mother, Edith, was making supper in the kitchen. Grandmother was knitting. Anne's older sister, Margot, sat tucked up on the sofa. When Anne tried to talk to her, she told her to go away.

Only the cat, Moortie, was still friendly. Anne picked her up and cuddled her.

"What's the matter, Moortie?" she asked. "Is it the Nazis?" The cat stared at Anne with deep green eyes and licked her hand.

"Dear Moortie!" Anne smiled. "Everything will be OK, won't it?"

Moortie carried on licking.

The next day, everyone was more cheerful.
At school, Anne's friends talked about the
trucks and the soldiers, but they were not
worried. By the time of her eleventh birthday,
on June 12, Anne had almost forgotten about
the Nazis. They were like a cloud that had
blotted out the sun for a while and then
blown away again.

By the spring, the cloud had returned.

One Saturday morning, Jan, Mary, and some of Anne's other classmates were talking about going to the movies. Anne liked Jan, a tall boy with a mop of straight fair hair.

"Great!" she cried. "Can I come?"

Mary stared at her.

"You? Of course not, Anne. Don't be silly." Anne felt her bottom lip trembling.

"Why not? I'm your friend, aren't I?"

"Of course you are," said Jan. "But you're a Jew, aren't you? Jews aren't allowed to go to the movies any more. Nazi orders."

Anne felt like crying and shouting and screaming all at the same time. She wanted to say how much she hated the Nazis and their stupid laws. But then she remembered the promise she'd made to her father.

With an effort, she looked Jan in the eye.

"Of course," she said slowly. "I don't want you to get into trouble for being with a Jew. Go to the movies without me. Anyway, I'm busy on Saturday," she added, trying to hide her disappointment.

The Nazi cloud grew thicker and darker. One morning that summer, Mrs. Frank came into Anne's room and sat on the edge of her bed. "I've news for you, Anne darling," she said. When she reached for her daughter's hand, Anne knew that the news was bad.

"Next semester, you and Margot will be going to a new school," said Mrs. Frank.

Anne's face fell. "But I don't want—"

"It's not a question of what you want, Anne," interrupted her mother. "It's the law. Jews are not allowed to go to school with Dutch children any more."

Life for the Jews in Germany was terrible by 1941. Most were rounded up and sent to concentration camps.

The Nazis and their Dutch supporters began treating the Dutch Jews the same way. They were banned from public places such as theaters, restaurants, and swimming pools. Later, Jews and non-Jews were not allowed to work together.

The Lucky One

Anne quickly settled into the Jewish Secondary
School. One of her best friends, Hanneli
Goslar, also went there. The teachers liked
Anne, and so did the other pupils. Peter Wessel,
a lad with a mischievous
gleam in his eye,
enjoyed bicycling home
with her through the
cobbled streets. He said
the way her glossy black
hair blew out behind
her reminded him of
a wild pony.

The winter of 1941–2 was long and hard. Because of the war, food was scarce and there was a lot of illness.

Shortly after Christmas, Anne's grandmother caught a chill. Within a week, she was dead.

Anne had loved her grandmother dearly – almost as much as her mother and father. Now, she felt as if a piece of her heart had broken off. Something her parents said upset her, too.

After the funeral, Anne heard her father say, "It's sad, Edith. But she may be the lucky one."

"I'm afraid you're right, Otto," Mrs. Frank sighed. "In some ways, I envy her."

Only later, when terrible things were happening, did Anne realize what her parents had meant.

Meanwhile, the laws against the Jews were
becoming stricter and stricter. Jews had to wear
a yellow Star of David sewn onto their clothes
so that everyone could recognize them. And
they were not allowed to go out after eight
o'clock at night.

One evening, Anne went for a walk with
her new boyfriend, Harry Goldberg.

When they arrived home ten minutes
late, Mr. Frank was waiting on the doorstep.
He was seething with anger.

"You silly girl!" he hissed. "Didn't you think
of the danger?"

Anne was confused. Then she noticed that
her father's eyes were fixed on something
across the road. She turned to see a pair
of soldiers standing in the shadows.
They were watching her closely.

Life for the Jews of Amsterdam had become even worse
by May 1942. They were not allowed to drive, use public
transportation or own a bike. They could shop for only two
hours a day, and only in stores with the sign "Jewish Shop".

Terrible news came from Germany. The Nazis had started to
kill the Jews in the concentration camps with poison gas.

Dear Kitty...

The summer started brilliantly.

Anne had a really good report from school. She managed to spend lots of time with Harry, playing ping-pong and going to one of the ice-cream parlors that was still open to Jews.

Best of all, for her thirteenth birthday her parents gave her a diary.

Anne loved writing. The diary, which she called Kitty, was soon her best friend – better even than Hanneli or Moortie. Whenever she had a quiet moment, she picked up her pen and began, "Dear Kitty... "

Only Kitty knew Anne's secret hopes and fears. Her biggest fear was what the Nazis would do next.

Mr. Frank shared his daughter's fear. One afternoon, when he was out walking with Anne and Margot, he suddenly turned to them and said, "You know we'll have to go into hiding soon, don't you?"

Anne looked at him in amazement.

"Hiding?" she asked. "Why on earth should we go into hiding, Daddy?"

"Because," he replied, "it's better to disappear before the Nazis come looking for us." He put an arm around her shoulder. "We should go before it's too late."

Anne nodded. "But when will we hide?" she asked. "And where?"

"Don't worry," her father replied. "Just enjoy yourself for the moment. You'll know when the time comes."

The time came sooner than Anne expected. Three days later, when she was reading a book on the balcony, the front door bell rang. Margot went to answer it.

Shortly afterward, she came rushing back upstairs. "It was Nazis," she panted. "They want Daddy. They're sending him to a work camp."

Although it was a hot July afternoon, Anne shivered. She knew what work camp meant. It meant a long journey to the east, starvation, and almost certain death. She couldn't believe it. Not her own father...

She spent the rest of the afternoon in a daze. Several of the family's Dutch friends came and went. Early that evening, Margot joined Anne in their room. The older girl's face was chalk white, and her hands were shaking, just like Grandmother's had done.

"Dearest Anne," she began, "I have something to tell you." She spoke automatically, like a machine they had heard long ago at a carnival. "I made a mistake. The Nazis were not asking for Daddy. They were asking for me. They want *me* to go to a work camp!"

Anne threw her arms around Margot's neck. "No!" she cried. "Not you! Not anyone! You're only 16. They can't take you away!"

Margot took out a handkerchief and dabbed her sister's eyes.

"No, of course they can't. Mother promised. Come on, Anne, we need to get packed. We're going into hiding. Now."

Now, Jews were not allowed to own or run businesses. The Nazis took over the businesses and gave them to others. Otto Frank had expected this to happen. He had already handed over his business to two Dutch friends, Victor Kugler and Johannes Kleiman, who were running it for him.

Into Hiding

Mrs. Frank woke Anne at dawn. She explained to her daughter that they could not take any luggage with them. The police would know that a Jew carrying a suitcase was trying to escape. Anne could take only her school satchel and the clothes she was wearing.

Anne had already crammed her satchel full of her favorite possessions, including Kitty. She now dressed as if she were going to the North Pole – two pairs of stockings, two camisoles, three pairs of panties, a dress, a skirt, a jacket, a coat, shoes, a wool cap and a scarf.

Feeling like a giant bear, Anne went to
the window and looked out. Thank goodness!
The hot weather had ended, and thin drizzle
was falling from a gray sky.

At seven-thirty, Anne said goodbye to
Moortie and followed her parents out into the
wet street. Although she had no idea where
they were going, she didn't mind. She knew
they would be safe.

At the moment, that was all that mattered.

The family made their way through
the city to the building where
Mr. Frank worked. Making sure
no one was watching, they
slipped inside and went
upstairs to the office.

They climbed another flight of stairs, turned right and — to Anne's amazement — they were suddenly inside the secret apartment that Mr. Frank had been preparing for his family.

For a time, Anne forgot her fear. It was such an adventure! Once she had unpacked her things and decorated her room with pictures of movie stars, she thought that her new home was the most comfortable hiding place in all of Holland. What's more, she had something to look forward to.

The Franks were to share their hideaway with the van Pels family. Peter van Pels was 15. Anne couldn't wait to meet him.

The Nazis were now rounding up Jews all over Holland. Many Dutch people risked their lives by helping them escape or go into hiding.

Several people working in the building knew about the Jews in the secret apartment. Victor Kugler and Johannes Kleiman knew. So did Miep and Jan Gies, and Bep Voskuijl and his father.

The Secret World

Through thin curtains, the autumn sunshine flooded into the small room. Anne, seated at the table, stared at the numbers in Mr. Kugler's book. She had to add up 25 columns, each with 32 numbers in it. What a bore!

But it was thanks to Mr. Kugler and his friends that they were still alive. Helping with their bookkeeping was the least she could do.

She took a deep breath and started to add the columns of figures. Five plus 32 equals 37, plus nine makes…

"Anne, have you brushed your hair this morning?" It was her mother's voice, nagging.

Anne felt anger rising within her. Still staring at the figures, she said slowly, "Mom, how many times do I have to tell you that I'm 13 now? I don't need a babysitter. I'm trying to work."

"I know that, dear," replied Mrs. Frank. "But just because we're in hiding, it doesn't mean we shouldn't take care of ourselves."

"Hear, hear!" chimed in Mrs. van Pels from the other side of the room.

Anne thought her head would explode.

"Leave me alone!" she muttered through gritted teeth. "We've been here more than a year, and all we do is argue. All day, every day. I hate it! I hate all of you! I want to run away."

She slammed down her pencil and stamped into the tiny room she shared with Margot. Throwing herself on her bed, she buried her face in her hands, sobbing loudly.

Everything had gone wrong. Peter had turned out to be boring. She badly missed her old friends, especially Hanneli. Now she had only Kitty to share her secrets with.

They were all trapped in the secret apartment, like chickens in a coop. They got on each other's nerves. They were short of food, soap, clothes, and terrified of the dreaded knock on the door…

Later, her father came talk to her. He spoke softly and kindly. He knew it was difficult, terribly difficult, to live like this. But at least they were alive and safe.

There was hope, too, he explained. In a short time – maybe in the next few months – British and American troops would cross the Channel and drive the Nazis from Holland. They must be patient. They had survived one year, so they could survive another.

Anne put her hand on her father's shoulder. "Do you believe that, Daddy? Do you really think we will be free soon?"

The seven Jews living in the secret apartment were joined on November 16, 1942, by an eighth, Fritz Pfeffer. They all did what they could to help their Dutch protectors. In addition to bookkeeping work, they filled gravy packets and took the stones out of cherries.

We Know Everything!

Fall dragged into winter, and winter into spring. Still the war raged on. And still the small group of Jews remained shut away from the world.

But now there was real hope. Everywhere, the Nazis were in retreat. The Russians were driving them back in the east and, step by step, they were being forced out of Italy.

Anne was more relaxed, too. As she neared her fifteenth birthday, she was fast becoming a young woman. She was annoyed when others still treated her as a child, but she learned not to react. Besides, she had a new joy in her life.

Over the long months together, she had come to see Peter in a different light. There was more to him than she had realized.
He was not as clever as her, but he was calmer.

She grew to like him more and more.

Peter was desperately shy. Day by day, sitting with him in the attic where he worked, she encouraged him to talk. And the more he talked, the fonder she became of him. In time, her fondness grew to love. She told Kitty that for the first time in years, she felt really happy.

In June came the wonderful news that British and American troops had landed in France. Freedom seemed only weeks away.

On the morning of August 4, Victor Kugler was disturbed by a loud knocking on his office door. Before he could answer, a group of armed men burst in. The leader wore the unmistakable uniform of a Nazi policeman.

"Don't say a word!" he barked. "We know everything. Take us to the Jews." Kugler hesitated. The Nazi raised his pistol. "Now, Mr. Kugler. No trouble, please."

Kugler led the way to the bookcase that hid the door to the secret apartment.

"It's behind there," he said. Two men pushed the bookcase aside.

At first, Anne thought it was a dream. There they all were – her parents, Margot, Mr. and Mrs. van Pels, Peter, and Mr. Pfeffer – standing with their backs to the wall, terrified. Had two years of miserable hiding really been in vain?

"Bring me all your valuables," ordered the policeman in his thick Austrian accent. Then he gave them five minutes to pack. "Your vacation is over," he added sarcastically. "It's time you joined the other Jews and did something useful."

Clutching her tattered satchel, Anne was hurried down the stairs and pushed toward a waiting truck. A small crowd had gathered on the street to see what was going on. As Anne passed, an old woman stepped forward and touched her lightly on the arm.

"Good luck, my dear," she whispered.

Before Anne could reply, she was bundled into the truck with the others and driven off to prison.

Before the war about 130,000 Jews lived in Holland. The Nazis killed 100,000 of them. They also made thousands of Dutch men and women work in German factories. The city of Amsterdam was not freed until May 1945.

Into the Night

It was now six months since the Franks had been captured. A bitter wind howled through the barbed-wire fence of Belsen concentration camp. Nearby, hundreds of women prisoners were crammed into a wooden hut. Sick and starving, they were stacked like garbage bags in filthy bunk beds.

The door creaked open. A girl entered and
looked about her. Pulling a thin shawl closer
around her bony shoulders, she knelt and
whispered to one woman, "Anne Frank?
Do you know where I can find Anne Frank?"
The old woman stared at her blankly for a
moment. Then she lifted an arm no thicker than
a stick and pointed to a far corner. The visitor
thanked her and shuffled across the room.

"Hanneli? Hanneli Goslar?" Anne's voice could scarcely be heard above the noise of the wind. "Is it really you? Why are you here?"

Hanneli forced herself to smile. "Yes, Anne darling, it's your old friend from Amsterdam. Look, I've brought you something." She placed a small package of food on the grimy straw of Anne's mattress.

When her friend stretched out a hand toward it, Hanneli saw that the thin fingers were covered in sores. "Tell me Hanneli, where am I?" Anne asked. "Is it Auschwitz?"

"No, my dear. They have moved you to another camp."

A look of pain came into Anne's eyes.

"But Mommy and Daddy are at Auschwitz. I want to see them." She made a sobbing sound, but no tears came.

Hanneli grasped her hand. "Don't cry, Anne. It will soon be over, and then you will be with them again."

Anne slowly closed her eyes. "Soon be over? Yes, thank God, it will soon be over."

Hanneli stayed with Anne until she was sure that she was asleep. Then, kissing her friend lightly on the forehead, she went out into the night.

The Frank family was taken first to Westerbork camp, then to the Auschwitz concentration camp. Here, the men and women were separated. At the end of October 1944, Anne and Margot, both seriously ill, were moved to Belsen. Margot died sometime in March, Anne just a few days later. British troops reached Belsen on April 15, 1945.

The Victims

Edith Frank, Anne's mother, died in Auschwitz on January 6, 1945. Mr. and Mrs. van Pels, Peter, and Mr. Pfeffer also died at the hands of the Nazis. Otto Frank, Anne's father, was the only one from the secret apartment to survive. The Russians rescued him from Auschwitz on January 27, 1945. It took him seven months to find out what had happened to Margot and Anne.

We do not know exactly how many Jews the Nazis killed during the war. It was probably about six million, the greatest slaughter in human history.

Anne Frank's Diary

After the Franks had been taken prisoner, Miep Gies went to the secret apartment and found Anne's diary. She kept it, hoping to give it back after the war. When she learned that Anne was dead, she gave it to Otto Frank. In 1947, he arranged for it to be published in Dutch. Since then, it has been translated into more than 50 languages and read by millions of people. Thanks to Anne's young talent, her memory and that of all the other victims of Nazi racism will live forever.

Timeline

1929 June 12   Anne Frank is born in Frankfurt, Germany.

1933   Frank family moves to Amsterdam, Holland, to escape from the Nazis.

1934   Anne starts school.

1940 May   The Nazis invade Holland.

1941   Margot and Anne move to the Jewish secondary school, Amsterdam.

1942 June 12   Anne receives Kitty, her diary, for her thirteenth birthday.

1942 July 6   The Frank family goes into hiding.

1944 August 4   Nazis discover the secret apartment and arrest everyone there.

Sept. 3   The eight Jews from the secret apartment are sent to Auschwitz concentration camp, Poland.

October   Margot and Anne are moved to Belsen concentration camp, Germany.

1945 January 6   Edith Frank dies.

January 27   The Russians free Otto Frank from Auschwitz.

March   Margot and Anne die.

1947   Anne's diary is published in Dutch.

1980   Otto Frank dies, aged 91.

More Information

Books to read
The Diary of a Young Girl by
Anne Frank, Penguin, 1997.
Anne Frank by John Rowley,
Heinemann, 1999.
Anne Frank by Harriet Castor,
Watts, 1996.
Anne Frank by Rachel Epstein,
Watts, 1997.
The Last Days of Freedom by Roy
Apps, Macdonald Young Books, 1998.

Websites
http://www.annefrank.nl
http://www.annefrank.com

Museum
Otto Frank's workplace at
263 Prinsengracht in Amsterdam is
now a museum called Anne Frank
House. Visitors can see the secret
apartment and many objects that
belonged to the eight people who
hid there.

Glossary

Auschwitz The largest Nazi
concentration camp, in Poland. The
Nazis killed one and a half million
people at Auschwitz, many with gas.

Belsen Also known as Bergen-
Belsen, this was a huge concentration
camp in northern Germany.

bookkeeping Writing down all the
money a business takes in and pays out.

concentration camp A large prison
made up of huts surrounded by high
fences of barbed wire.

Nazi The Nazis ruled Germany
from 1933 to 1945. Their leader
was Adolf Hitler. He believed that
all Jews were evil. Hitler's supporters
organized the deaths of about
six million Jews.

Star of David The six-pointed
star that is the symbol of the Jewish
people. The Nazis made all Jews
wear a Star of David so they
could be recognized.

work camp The Nazi name
for a concentration camp.

Index